Charming DOLLS

Make Cloth Dolls with Personality Plus

Easy Visual Guide to Painting, Stitching, Embellishing & More

----

Shirley Hudson

C&T PUBLISHING

Text, photography, and artwork copyright © 2021 by Shirley Hudson

Publisher: Amy Barrett-Daffin

Creative Director: Gailen Runge

Acquisitions Editor: Roxane Cerda

Managing/Developmental Editor: Liz Aneloski

Technical Editor: Debbie Rodgers

Cover/Book Designer: April Mostek

Production Coordinator: Tim Manibusan

Production Editor: Jennifer Warren

Illustrators: Shirley Hudson and Mary E. Flynn

Photo Assistant: Lauren Herberg

Cover photography by Shirley Hudson

Photography by Selina Hudson, unless otherwise noted

Published by C&T Publishing, Inc., P.O. Box 1456, Lafayette, CA 94549

Library of Congress Cataloging-in-Publication Data

Names: Hudson, Shirley Cowan, 1967- author.

Title: Charming dolls : make cloth dolls with personality plus : easy visual guide to painting, stitching, embellishing & more / Shirley Hudson.

Description: Lafayette, CA : C&T Publishing, [2021]

Identifiers: LCCN 2020056204 | ISBN 9781644031186 (trade paperback) | ISBN 9781644031193 (ebook)

Subjects: LCSH: Dollmaking. | Cloth dolls.

Classification: LCC TT175 .H825 2021 | DDC 745.592/21--dc23

LC record available at https://lccn.loc.gov/2020056204

Printed in the USA

10 9 8 7 6 5 4 3 2 1

DEDICATION

To my daughter, Selina, and my husband, Dana, my true eternal loves!

ACKNOWLEDGMENTS

I want to thank my sisters, Angie, Cecilia, and Julie, and my brother, Vince, for all the fun, great times we had growing up. There was never a dull moment! Imagination was our greatest asset—no matter what supplies or how little money we had, we all made the most of it. Each one of you brought something different to the table. Childhood would never have been so wonderful if I didn't have all of you! I am thankful for you all.

I also want to thank my great friend Sue. You are the best! You are so talented, and you always make the most amazing dolls. You make me laugh all the time, you inspire me, and I treasure our times together. A big shout-out to all my friends at the craft shows, quilt shows, and doll club, too!

I want to give a special thank-you to my daughter, Selina, who took almost all the photos for this book. You are very talented! You have so many ideas and tackled them all. I couldn't have done this without you! Hugs and kisses!

CONTENTS

INTRODUCTION

For thousands of years, women have been making dolls for their children to play with. As kids we played and played, often until our dolls became torn and tattered. Sometimes the fascination for dolls never leaves us, even as we mature and grow older. Dolls are so much more than a toy—they lift our spirits, remind us of simpler times, drive our imaginations, and liven up our home decor.

Making art dolls is a passion of mine. Art dolls are not made for children but for people who are children at heart, like you and me! There are no rules and no right way to make them. Be playful and experiment; try something new and different. Let go of perfectionism! As children, we made art from pure joy and experimentation. Now is the time to find that spirit again. Art dolls should come from your imagination, so get out of your comfort zone and let loose!

I began making Halloween dolls because I really love the holiday. As a child, it meant free candy, fun, and an escape from the usual homework and duties. I learned many crafting skills over the years, including how to use common, easy-to-find materials and make them special. My first doll of this kind was a goofy witch. She was cute, and I was hooked!

In this book, you will learn how to sew primitive playful doll shapes, paint faces with ease, use several mediums for extra texture, and embellish. The sky's the limit!

SUPPLIES

Muslin: Plain muslin is the base for all the dolls' heads and torsos. This simple beige fabric is perfect to sew and paint on, and the muslin will not be visible when the doll is complete.

Fabric scraps for the arms, legs, and backing: Any cotton fabric is good. Pick fabrics that will go with your doll or complement it. Consider holiday fabrics, vintage floral sheets, modern designs, white on white, fabric that looks like animal print, plaids, stripes, denim, and batik. Check your stash of scraps!

Pencil: Use a plain ordinary pencil, not a mechanical one.

Black thread: Black thread is used for primitively stitching the dolls; it is part of the playful, cute look. Other thread colors get lost in the painting process. Use matching thread for the arms and legs.

Walking foot / quilting foot: This foot is perfect for free-motion stitching. Most sewing machines now have this attachment. If your machine doesn't, you can also sew with a regular sewing foot; however, a regular sewing foot doesn't have the same playful stitching capabilities.

Sewing machine: Any sewing machine will do. I don't recommend that these dolls be stitched by hand.

Scissors: Sharp fabric scissors are best.

EZ Point & Turner (by Sue O'Very Designs; Famoré Cutlery) or safety pin: Turning arms and legs right side out is much easier with these tools.

Polyfil stuffing and stuffing tool: The dolls do not use a lot of stuffing. Many bags of stuffing come with a wooden stuffing tool.

Acrylic paints in a variety of colors: Most brands of paint are very similar to each other. Use what you like.

Paint brushes in 2 or 3 sizes: Use small brushes for details and large ones for spreading out more paint.

Palette or paper plate: It is important to keep your paints separate, especially when watering down the paint.

Pastels: I use the Cray-Pas 25-color set (by Sakura Color Products Corp.). Inexpensive pastels are perfect. Pastels add great color that is much more dramatic than colored pencils.

Colored pencils (at least 24): Colored pencils are easy to use, especially in small areas. The color can be light or intensified with layering.

Pencil sharpener: Keep your colored pencils sharp!

Fixative spray: I use Workable Fixatif (by Krylon), a spray that sets paint, colored pencils, and pastels. The spray protects the doll's face and torso from smudges. It can be found at most grocery superstores and craft stores.

Hot glue gun and sticks: Hot glue is the easiest and quickest way to attach arms and legs, add embellishments, and more. Any kind and brand are good.

Ribbons, trims, yarns, and lace: Scraps of these are perfect for dolls. Check your stash!

Embellishments: You can use ephemera, buttons, tulle, glitter, clear tacky glue, old jewelry, flowers, wool, sticks, straw, wool, felt, and the like.

DOLL BASICS

The basics provide all the steps in creating the art dolls.
Feel free to use your own creativity, too.

Draw the Doll on Muslin

1. There are several pattern pieces for the dolls in this book. Choose the appropriate ones for the doll you want to make.

NOTE ■ Drawing your own designs on paper or directly on muslin is highly encouraged. You can use my patterns as a guide to draw your own doll designs. Draw your custom patterns on paper first so you can erase, add new lines, and change as you go. Remember that the doll will be stuffed later. If the head is skinny now, it will be even skinnier when stuffed!

2. Press the muslin flat.

3. Cut the muslin pieces about 1″ larger than the doll pattern on all sides. This makes it easier to pull and push the fabric as you are free-motion sewing.

4. Trace the doll pattern onto paper and cut it out. Lay the pattern piece down and trace all the way around the shape with a pencil. The pencil line is your sewing line.

5. Choose a backing fabric for your doll; fun fabrics that match the theme of your doll are best. The backing fabric should be the same size as the front of the doll. Place the muslin with the traced doll shape on top of the backing fabric, wrong sides together. Pin in place.

Primitive Sewing: Head and Body

Thread the sewing machine with black thread and use black thread in the bobbin. Always sew on the traced line.

There are two ways to sew the dolls.

Option 1: Using a Free-Motion Foot

For primitive free-motion sewing, use a walking foot or quilting foot with the feed dogs down or a darning plate covering the feed dogs.

Sew primitively, with at least a total of 3 sewing lines going over each other. It is a back-and-forth technique. Sew forward ¾″ or 1″; then sew backwards over the stitched area or near it. Sew forward again over the previous stitches and another 1″. Repeat around the doll shape. It is perfectly fine, and encouraged, to sew over or beside other lines. This allows for a playful look with rough edges.

Option 2: Using a Standard Sewing Foot

Using a standard sewing foot with the feed dogs up, sew around the traced doll shape 3 times in a playful manner, being a little sloppy. Let the sewing lines go over and around each other somewhat. Be imperfect!

Free-motion stitching: Stitch back and forth over traced line.

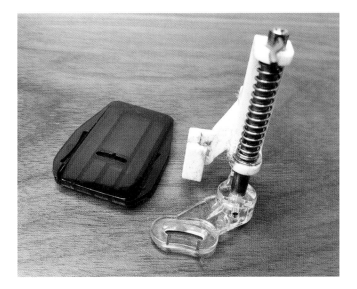

Regular stitching: Stitch over traced line 3 times.

Finish Sewing the Head and Body

1. Leave a 2 or 3″ opening at the bottom of the doll.

2. The doll will not be turned inside out. Trim away the excess muslin ⅛″–¼″ from the sewn lines.

3. Stuff the doll head firmly, especially in the neck section. Stuff the torso last.

4. Pin and sew the opening closed; stitch it primitively as before.

Tips

- *Sew the hair strands of the hair that are outside the normal circular shape of the head. Bangs and parts in hair can be painted.*

- *When sewing the ears on the cats, sew the ear shape and then around the circular part of the head. The ears will be not stuffed.*

Base of the Head, Hair, and Body

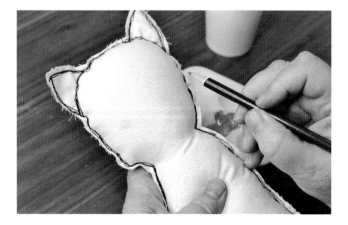

1. Mark the placement of the eyes, nose, and mouth lightly with a pencil.

2. If it is a boy or girl, mark the placement of the bangs or the top of the hair with a pencil. This is temporary and will help you know how you want the face to look. The pair of eyes should be placed down in the center of the face, leaving a large forehead/hair area. Wide-set eyes look lovely.

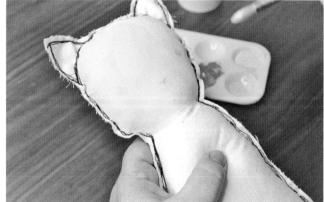

3. Gather a cup of water, a palette, paint, and brushes.

4. The first step in painting the dolls is adding a face color. Add paint to the palette and dip your medium/large brush into the water. Let the water drip into the paint on the palette. Stir the paint. Acrylic paint can be thick, and water thins it out nicely.

5. Paint the face, neck, and ears.

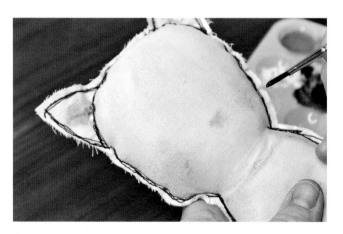

6. While the face is still wet, add cheeks in a slightly watered-down pink paint. The wet paints will blend nicely together. Blend with your finger to soften the color, if needed. Also add a little pink to the nose area and mouth. Let the face dry.

7. If your doll has hair, paint the hair and bangs with lightly watered-down paint. Paint in the stitched area of the hair too. Let dry.

8. Paint the torso/body of the doll in the color of your choice. The torso might be the doll's outfit or clothes, or it might be the animal's fur. Paint accordingly. Let dry.

Edges of the Dolls

1. The raw edges of the doll, from the sewn line outward, can be plain cream-colored muslin or painted black. Both options are nice—it's just a matter of preference.

2. To paint the edges, water down the black paint: 1 part paint, 1 part water. Stir. Paint the edges of the doll from the stitched line outward. Let dry.

Eyes, Nose, Mouth, and Hair

There are a several types of eyes used in this book. The eye-painting guides will make the process much simpler.

Eyes

THE STANDARD EYE

1. Start the eye by painting a large black circle. It is the outermost part of all the eyes. Play with the size of the circle—small eyes are just as nice as large ones. Dolls featured in this book have ½″–⅝″ black circular eyes. Let dry between steps.

2. Paint a slightly smaller iris circle over the black circle. Let dry.

3. Paint a black pupil in the center of the eye. Let dry.

4. Paint a large dot in the upper right side with white. This is a highlight. Paint a white curved line in the lower left side, between the iris and the outer black circle. Let dry.

5. Add flecks of color in the iris by taking a lighter or darker shade of colored pencil and drawing some lines in the iris, from near the pupil towards the outer eye.

CAT'S EYES LOOKING UPWARD AND COY

Paint the cat eyes following the eye painting guide below.

• Paint a black circle. Let dry.

• Paint a small semicircle to create an iris. Let dry.

• Add white highlights to the eye. Let dry.

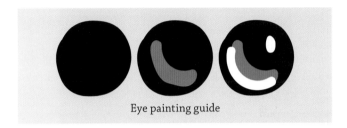
Eye painting guide

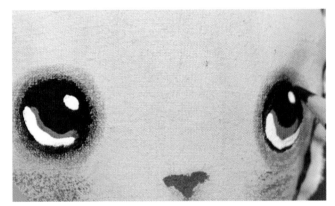
Follow the diagram.

Nose

1. Paint a flat oval with pink paint. Allow the paint to spread a little above the nose.

2. Add a curved line above the nose with yellow paint. This creates the tip of the nose. Let dry.

3. Add extra pink and yellow using colored pencils.

4. Tan/brown colored pencils are wonderful for shading around the outside of the nostrils. A gentle touch of black colored pencil is perfect for nostrils. Use it around the outer curve of the nose and the ball (bottom tip of the nose).

5. Use a white pastel for a shine or highlight on the nose.

Animal noses can be shaped like a triangle with nostrils.

Mouth

1. For a basic mouth, small pink lips are best.

2. Add white pastel on the lips to create a slight shine.

3. Using a black colored pencil, draw a smile on the lips.

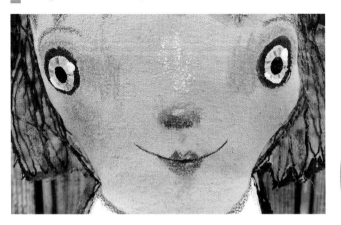

Tip

Animals usually only need a slight pinkish area near the mouth. Use a black colored pencil for the line coming down from the nose to the mouth. Add whiskers with a black colored pencil when you are finished with the entire face.

Hair Details

Your doll's hair color should not be a flat color of paint. Colored pencils and pastels will add interest to hair. Try adding lines or strands of hair in different tones and colors—use lighter shades and darker shades. Create a part in the hair using darker colors. Outline the hairline with colored pencils. Add white pastel to the hair, as if the sun's light is bouncing off of it.

Tip: Shading

Shading makes your doll less flat and more like a real person. When shading your doll, imagine the sun above your doll, and choose which side you would like the sun to shine down on. Place a cup on the table where the sun would be to remind you. Everything the sun would be casting down its rays on should be light, not shadow. There can also be a highlight of white for a shine. Everywhere that would have a shadow can have darker shades added to it. Shadows could be on the side of the face, nose, inner eye areas, under the bottom lip, under the nose, and so on.

Add Layers of Color to the Head

Just a layer or two of paint can look pretty boring. Adding layers of colored pencils and pastels really livens up your doll. When adding these two mediums, lines and strokes of color are best.

Colored pencils tend to give a lighter touch and are much more subtle. It is much easier to start light and add to it rather than start with a heavy hand.

Pastels are thicker and richer, and give a deeper look to colors. Pastels are perfect to add to hair, the torso, or the painted outfits and highlights in white.

Tip

Blue and green colored pencils are essential for showing the curvature or roundness of an otherwise flat surface. Add these colors on the sides of the faces and near the side of the nose and mouth. These colors seem crazy to add to a girl's face, but it looks really good!

Eyebrows

Use colored pencils to draw the eyebrows. Use pastels if you want thicker brows.

Extra Color on the Torso

1. Add design and color to the torso area by adding pastels. Try polka dots, stripes, pockets, fur lines (for animals), plaid, zigzag lines, and stars.

2. To set all of the paint, colored pencils, and pastels, spray the head and torso with fixative spray. Let dry. Spray again if needed.

Arms and Legs

1. Think about how you want your doll to look, and pick out fabric for the arms and legs accordingly. Arms should match or blend with the torso. Legs can also be pants or stockings. Long stripes look great for a boy doll or witch. Arms and legs on animals can be one fabric or color. Flowery fabric also looks great.

2. Trace the arm and leg patterns for your doll onto scrap paper. Cut them out.

3. Place the arm pattern on the wrong side of the fabric and trace around the pattern with a pencil. Repeat for the other arm, leaving at least ½″ between them. The traced line is the sewing line.

4. Place the traced arms on top of another piece of fabric, right sides together, and pin.

5. Repeat the same process for the legs.

6. Using a regular sewing foot, sew on the traced lines of the arms and legs, leaving the ends open.

7. Trim excess fabric ¼″ around the sewn lines. Clip the curves and turn right side out.

8. Stuff the arms and legs only halfway.

9. Add the hands and feet/shoes by simply painting the ends of the arms or legs.

10. Hot glue the arms and legs closed near opening.

11. Hold the arms up to the body. Glue the arms to the back by the shoulder. Decide if you like your arms shorter or longer, and glue them to the back of the doll where you like.

12. Hold the legs up to the bottom back of your doll. Decide if you want shorter or longer legs. If your doll is mainly going to sit, try that position out before gluing. Hot glue the tops of the legs to the bottom back of your doll.

Optional: Cover the back of the doll, where the arms and legs are glued on, with trims or lace.

Embellishing

Embellishing is the best part of the whole doll process! The doll is looking great, and these are the final steps for completion. Flip through the pages of this book to get ideas and inspiration!

Add skirts of lace or tulle, pockets, collars, trims near the cuffs or by the feet, pins, flowers, and more!

Look in your stash of crafts to see what you already have. You can use old jewelry, crocheted flowers or bow ties, felt hearts, fun ephemera paper, ribbons, mini signs to hold or put into pockets, capes, pom-poms, yarns, fringy strings, buttons, glitter, strips of cheesecloth, rickrack, and tulle bows.

Add tails to animals using fabric (made like an arm or leg) or ribbon.

Holiday embellishments are great, too! Embellish with small Easter eggs or chicks in a basket, leaves and plastic spiders for fall, glittery garland for Christmas, gold coins for Saint Patrick's Day, a flag for a patriotic doll, and so much more.

Attach your embellishments to your doll with hot glue, stitches, safety pins, ties, or pin backs, or use a rubber band. Be playful!

Add a pocket to the doll by hot gluing both sides and the bottom of the pocket to the torso or add with stitches. Leave the top open. Easy peasy!

Hot glue lace on the doll for a fun, easy skirt. Gather up tulle with a running stitch and make an easy dress.

Tie on ribbons around the neck, on top of the hair, and/or around the hands and feet.

Add glitter to make a doll frosty, to add some sparkle, or to jazz up any area of the doll. It is simple to add glitter: Using clear-drying glue, spread glue on the areas you want to glitter up. Sprinkle glitter and shake off the excess. Let dry.

Adding signs for the dolls to hold is so much fun! Cut a stick or a drinking straw into a 4″-long piece. Gather pretty papers, sayings, buttons, felt ephemera, bits of party streamers, and more. Arrange them in a pleasing manner and hot glue to the stick or straw. Add ribbon or string for a bow. Hot glue or safety pin in place.

Cute coy kitty
Photo by Shirley Hudson

Photo by Shirley Hudson

HOLLY HOLIDAYS
Girl Doll with Accessories

Celebrate all the holidays and special days throughout the year with this sweet little girl. Her colors are white and sparkly gold, with a darling tulle dress. There are fourteen different accessories (page 25) she can hold in her lap. Change it up anytime!

Materials

Muslin: 8˝ × 11˝, plus a fat quarter for handheld accessories

Coordinating fabric scraps for arms and legs: 8˝ × 10˝ for each set

Fabric scrap for back of doll: 8˝ × 11˝, plus scraps for backs of accessories

White glittery tulle: 6˝ × 60˝

White perle cotton thread

Lace scraps: 1½˝ × 12˝

Gold trims: 14˝ total

Pencil

Black thread

Stuffing for dolls and stuff-it tool

Acrylic paint: Flesh, pink, yellow, white, black, and green for doll; variety of colors for accessories

Paintbrushes: Large and small

Colored pencils: Green, pink, yellow, gray, lighter blue, black, and brown

Pastels: White and yellow

Hot glue gun and glue sticks

Buttons: 1 large white and 2 small white

Paper flowers: 3 gold glitter with gems in the center

Fixative spray

Drawing the Doll

Refer to Draw the Doll on Muslin (page 8).

1. Make a paper pattern using the Holly Holidays Girl Doll body pattern (page 29). Place it on the muslin and trace with a pencil all the way around.

2. Place the traced muslin doll onto the backing fabric, wrong sides together, and pin. Trim the backing as needed.

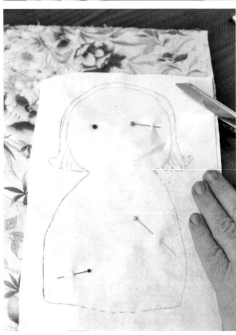

Finished doll:
7˝ × 14⅝˝

Finished accessories:
From 2⅜˝ × 2˝ to 4˝ × 2½˝

Photo by Shirley Hudson

Sewing the Doll

Refer to Primitive Sewing: Head and Body (page 9).

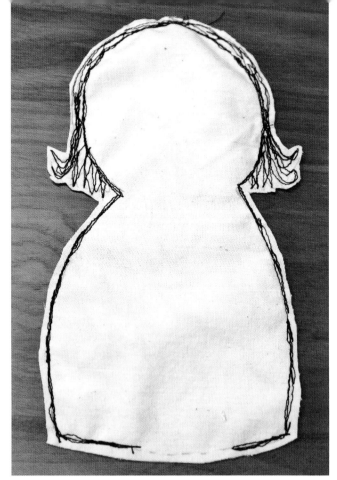

1. Primitively sew the head and body on the traced line around the doll shape, leaving a 3˝ opening at the bottom of the doll. Sew strands of hair outside of the circular head shape. Trim around the girl doll ⅛˝ away from the sewing line.

2. Stuff the girl doll firmly, especially in the neck area. Sew the opening on the girl doll closed.

3. Lightly mark the facial features (eyes, nose, mouth, and hair) with a pencil.

The Base of the Head and Body

Refer to Base of the Head, Hair, and Body (page 10).

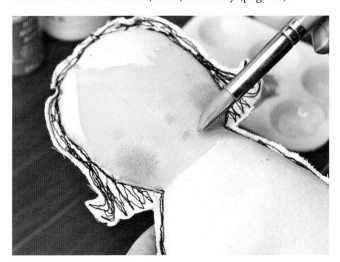

1. Paint the girl's face using a lightly watered-down flesh color. Leave the hair area with bangs alone. While the face is still wet, add pink to the cheeks. Add a small amount of pink to the nose area and mouth. The pink color will blend into the face color, creating a soft look. Let dry.

2. Paint the girl's hair a dark yellow, including between the sewn strands.

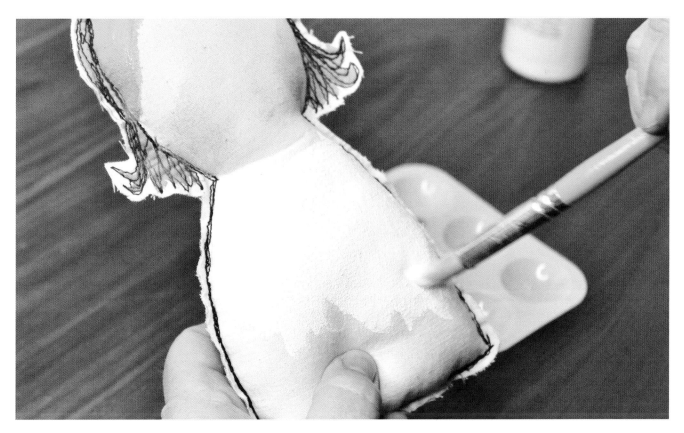

3. Paint her torso white. Let dry.

The Face

Refer to Eyes, Nose, Mouth, and Hair (page 11).

1. Paint the eyes following the eye painting guide below.

• Paint a black circle. Let dry.

• Paint a smaller green circle to create an iris. Let dry.

• Paint a small black circle for a pupil and a heavy line over the eye. Let dry.

• Add white highlights to the eye. Let dry.

• Add flecks of color in the iris with a lighter green colored pencil.

2. Paint the nose following the nose painting guide at right.

• Paint the nose as a flattened oval shape with pink paint.

• Paint above and on the sides of the nose with lightly watered-down pink paint.

• Paint the top of the nose with watered-down yellow paint.

3. Paint the mouth following the mouth painting guide at right.

• Paint the mouth pink.

Eye painting guide

Nose painting guide

Mouth painting guide

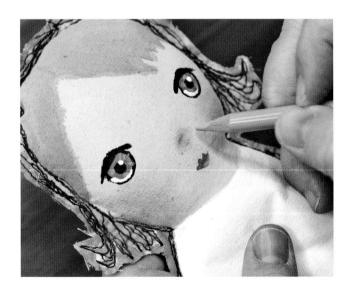

4. Add pink and yellow to the nose using colored pencils for more intense color.

5. Using a gray colored pencil, shadow under the ball of the nose. Add the outer part of the nose with blue colored pencil.

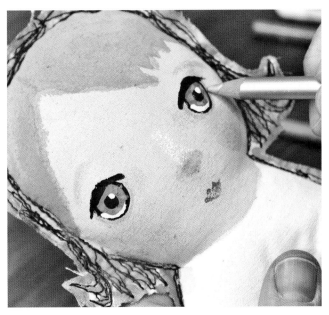

6. Add white pastel to the bridge of the nose as a highlight. If you made a mistake on the face (a mark from a pencil or too much colored pencil), take a flesh-colored pastel and cover the mistake. Painting over the mistake is also an option. Add a tiny amount of white pastel to the lips—this creates a highlight or sheen. Refer to Tip: Shading (page 12).

7. Add yellow to the inner areas of the eyes with a colored pencil, creating a shadow. Add eyebrows using a yellow colored pencil. Use a gray colored pencil under and on the sides of the eyes.

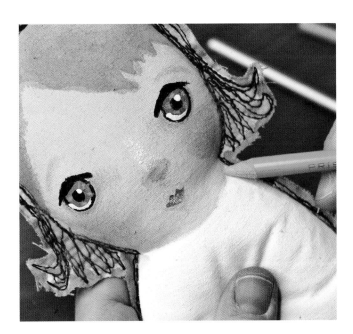

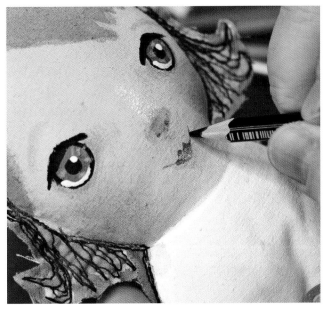

8. Using a yellow colored pencil, shadow under the lips. Apply a blue colored pencil to the innermost area of the eyes, around the nostrils, and by the side of the mouth. Layering these colors is a key to making the doll face lovely. Using blue colored pencil, shadow around the face, hairline, and neck.

9. Using black colored pencil, add nostrils and shadows under the nose. Also draw a line on the lips for a smile. Add shadowing around the eye, too.

10. Use yellow pastel to draw in streaks of color on the hair. Don't forget the strands by her neck!

11. Add brown and black to the hair using colored pencils. These shades will make the hair more realistic.

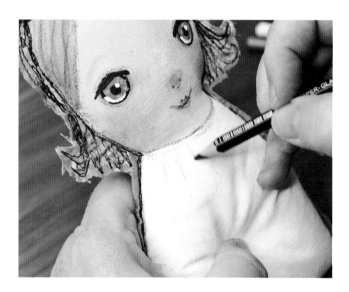

12. Apply brown colored pencil to the top of the eyelid.

13. Add shading around the neck and white top using a black colored pencil. Draw lines to give the top a gathered look.

14. Apply pink colored pencil to the lips and cheeks. Add more color to any parts of the face as desired.

15. Spray with fixative to set the paint, pencil, and pastel.

Sewing the Arms and Legs

Refer to Arms and Legs (page 14).

1. Make the arms and legs for the girl doll. Coordinating fabric choices are best.

2. Hot glue the arms and legs to the girl doll.

3. Paint the girl's hands a skin color and the feet black to resemble a shoe. Let dry.

Finishing Holly Holidays Girl Doll

Refer to Embellishing (page 15).

1. Hot glue lace to the doll's torso as a base for her dress.

2. For the skirt, fold a 60˝ piece of tulle in half. Thread a needle with white perle cotton and sew a loose running stitch along the long edge, ½˝ from the edge. Gather up the tulle.

3. Tie the tulle skirt to the doll over the smaller lace. The open end of the skirt should be toward the back. Hot glue in place.

4. Hot glue gold trim over the tulle skirt and around the hands.

5. Hot glue a big button near the neckline and a small button on each shoe. Hot glue gold flowers to her head.

Photo by Shirley Hudson

GIRL DOLL'S HANDHELD ACCESSORIES

There are fourteen different objects your girl doll can hold in her lap. They are simple yet sweet.

1. Trace the flower onto a scrap of paper and cut out. Refer to Draw the Doll on Muslin (page 8).

2. Trace the design onto muslin with a pencil.

3. Place the traced muslin on top of the backing fabric with wrong sides together. Pin in place.

4. Primitively sew around the shape, leaving no opening. Refer to Primitive Sewing: Head and Body (page 9).

5. Trim around the shape with scissors, ⅛˝ away from the sewing lines.

6. Cut a small slit in the back of the shape. Stuff lightly and sew the slit shut.

7. Paint with lightly watered-down paint. The flower has a yellow center and pink for the petals. Let dry. Refer to Base of the Head, Hair, and Body (page 10).

8. Add colored pencils and pastels to give extra colors and dimension. A smudge of white pastel in the center of the flower gives a nice highlight or shine to it. To define the center of the flower, add scribbled circles between the petals and center with black colored pencil. Refer to Tip: Shading (page 12).

Other Accessories

Snowman: Paint the snowman white; let dry. Using a variety of colored pencils, add a nose, cheeks, eyes, mouth, scarf, and heart on the chest. Shade the sides of snowman with gray pastels. Outline the carrot nose with black colored pencil.

Heart: Paint it red. Add red pastel to areas for more intense color.

Shamrock: Paint it green. Add green pastel to areas for more intense color.

Easter egg: Paint it yellow, pink, and orange. The colors can run into each other. Add pastels for more intense colors.

Bunny: Paint the bunny white. Let dry. Add the eyes, nose, mouth, ear color, and cheeks using colored pencils. Add shading for the bunny using gray pastel. Highlight the eyes with white paint. Outline the nose a little using black colored pencil.

Rainbow: Paint the rainbow using red, yellow, green, blue, and purple. Let the colors run into each other a little. Let dry. Add pastels to the rainbow for more color. Define some rainbow color changes by drawing dashed lines with a black colored pencil.

Coffee/tea: Paint the cup pink. Apply brown colored pencil to the inside of the cup for tea or coffee. Add pink pastel to the bottom of the cup to create a small shadow.

Flag: Paint the upper left corner blue. Paint red stripes. Let dry. Paint white stripes. Let dry. Add white paint star dots to the blue corner.

Sun: Paint the sun yellow. Let dry. Using colored pencils, add the eyes, smile, and cheeks. Add a white highlight to the sun's eyes. Add shades of yellow and orange to the sun's rays with pastels.

Pumpkin: Paint the pumpkin orange and the stem green. Let dry. Paint black eyes on the pumpkin. Let dry. Add a smile using black colored pencil. Add pastels for more intense colors. Highlight the eyes with a white paint dot. Add cheeks using pink colored pencil.

Photo by Shirley Hudson

Turkey: Paint the turkey brown. Let dry. Paint the feathers orange and yellow. Paint the beak yellow and the waddle red. Let dry. Using brown colored pencil, draw a wing. Add an eye using a black colored pencil and a white highlight in the eye using white paint. Add pastels for more color on the turkey.

Christmas tree: Paint the tree green and the star yellow. Let dry. Using colored pencils, add a tree trunk, ornaments, and pine branches. Use yellow pastel for more intense color on the star.

Bear: Paint the bear light brown/tan. Add the eyes, nose, and mouth using a black colored pencil. Add white highlights to the bear's eyes. Use a pink colored pencil for the cheeks. Add pastels for shadows on the bear's neck and body.

Rainbow

Sun

Christmas tree

Bunny

Heart

Pumpkin

Turkey

Bear

Flag

Shamrock

Egg

Coffee/tea

Snowman

Flower

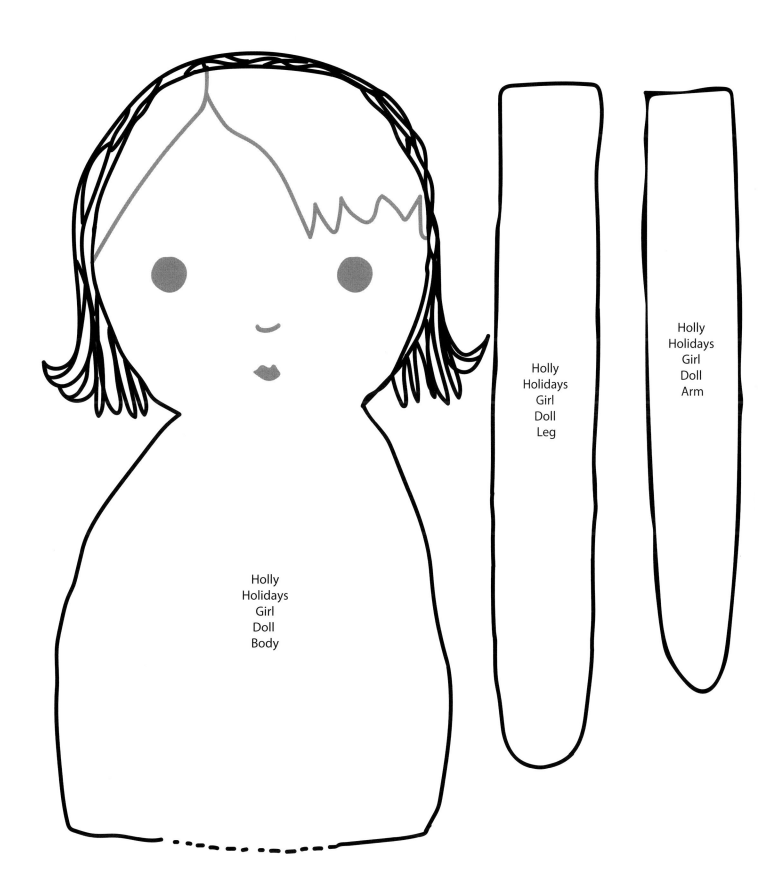

Holly
Holidays
Girl
Doll
Leg

Holly
Holidays
Girl
Doll
Arm

Holly
Holidays
Girl
Doll
Body

DaISY THE BUNNY

Hopping through the forest is a pretty little white bunny. She spends her time at tea parties with her crown of flowers and a few snacks in her pocket. Every afternoon is a perfect time to chat with the girls and show off their latest attire. Daisy is in the center of it all!

Materials

Muslin: 8″ × 12″

Coordinating fabric scraps for arms and legs: 8″ × 10″ for each set (I used vintage fabric sheets.)

Fabric scrap for back of doll: 8″ × 12″

Fabric scrap for pocket

Lace and ruffle scraps

Green tulle scraps

Orange wool/felt scraps

Pencil

Black thread

Stuffing for dolls and stuff-it tool

Acrylic paint: White, pink, gray, black, and brown

Paintbrushes: Large and small

Colored pencils: Brown, gray, black, yellow, pink, blue, and green

Pastels: White, pink, and gray

Hot glue gun and glue sticks

Button: 1 large pink

Paper flowers and stems for head

Pom-pom: 1 large pink for tail

Fixative spray

Drawing the Doll

Refer to Draw the Doll on Muslin (page 8).

1. Make a paper pattern using the Daisy the Bunny body pattern (page 37). Place it on the muslin and trace with a pencil all the way around.

2. Place the traced muslin doll onto the backing fabric, wrong sides together, and pin.

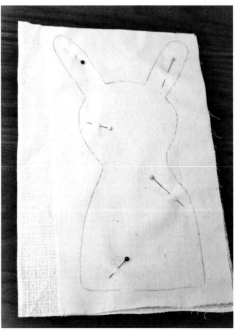

Finished doll:
7″ × 16½″

Sewing the Doll

Refer to Primitive Sewing: Head and Body (page 9).

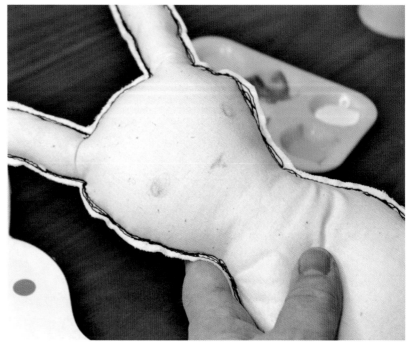

1. Primitively sew the head and body on the traced line around the bunny shape, leaving a 3″ opening at the bottom of the doll.

2. Trim around the bunny doll ⅛″ away from the sewing line.

3. Stuff the bunny doll firmly, especially in the neck area. Sew the opening on the bunny doll closed.

4. Lightly mark the facial features (eyes and nose) with a pencil.

The Base of the Head and Body

Refer to Base of the Head, Hair, and Body (page 10).

1. Paint the bunny's face, ears, and torso using a lightly watered-down white. While the face is still wet, add pink to the cheeks. Add a small amount of pink to the nose area and mouth. The pink color will blend into the white, creating a soft look. Let dry.

2. Apply watered-down gray paint to the outer edges of bunny, near the stitched lines. This creates depth. Also add gray to under the face by the neckline.

The Face

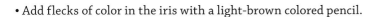

Refer to Eyes, Nose, Mouth, and Hair (page 11).

1. Paint the eyes following the eye painting guide below.

- Paint a black circle. Let dry.

- Paint a smaller brown circle to create an iris. Let dry.

- Paint a small black circle for a pupil. Let dry.

- Add white highlights to the eye. Let dry.

- Add flecks of color in the iris with a light-brown colored pencil.

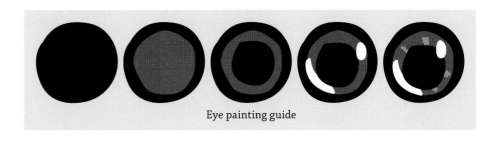

Eye painting guide

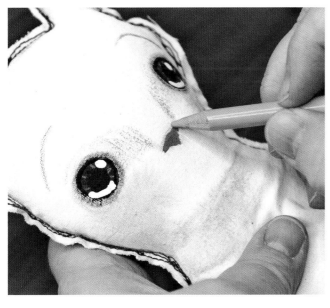

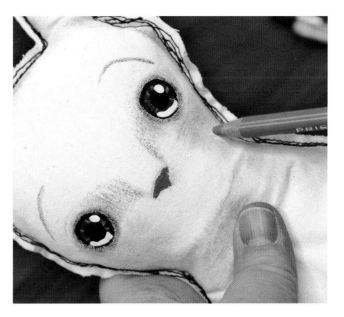

2. Paint the nose pink.

3. Apply gray colored pencil around the eyes. Also add black around the eyes using a colored pencil. Draw on eyebrows using black colored pencil. Gray pastels are fun to use on the face for nose definition.

4. Lightly apply yellow colored pencils to the inner and outer areas of the eyes. Add gray to the sides of the nose bridge and the shadow between the eyes and nose using a colored pencil. Apply yellow colored pencil to the top of the pink nose.

5. Add more cheek color using pink colored pencils.

Tip: Layering Colors

Colored pencils are a wonderful art tool. The doll faces will really pop if you gently add a layer of color and then add to it with more colors or the same color. Add shadows to the face by darkening the area with gray or black colored pencils.

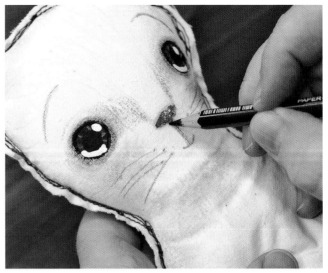

6. Apply pink colored pencil to the inner ears. Draw a line from the nose down to the mouth using pink colored pencil.

7. Add white pastel to the nose to create a shine.

8. Draw fur by making quick lines on the head using gray colored pencil.

9. Draw gray dots on cheeks near the mouth to create an area for the whiskers to come out of the fur. Using a black colored pencil, draw over the pink line from the nose to the mouth and draw a small smile.

10. Add nostrils and shadows under the nose with black colored pencil. Draw the whiskers in black.

Sewing the Arms and Legs

Refer to Arms and Legs (page 14).

1. Make the arms and legs for the bunny doll.

2. Hot glue the arms and legs to the bunny doll.

11. Add gray pastel to the body and ears to create fur. Shadow under the neck too.

12. Using blue colored pencil, add lines to the sides of the nose, by the inner eyes, to the sides of the head, and to the collar area. Blue and green create a feeling of curvature; this will make the face look more rounded.

13. Spray with fixative to set the paint, pencil, and pastel.

Finishing Daisy the Bunny

Refer to Embellishing (page 15).

Tip: Skirt Ideas
Easy skirts for dolls include lace, premade ruffles, tulle and fabric gathered by a running stitch, trims, and strips of fabric flowing down from the waist area.

1. Gather your supplies. Look around for fun things to add to your bunny doll.

2. Hot glue a pink ruffle around the lower waist of the bunny doll. Place the ends on the back.

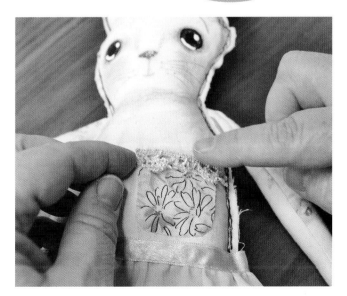

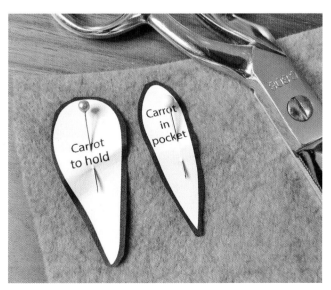

3. Cut 1 pocket from floral fabric and hot glue it onto the bunny just above the skirt, leaving the top open. Add lace trim to the top of the pocket using hot glue.

4. Using the 2 patterns for the carrots, cut out both carrots from orange wool/felt.

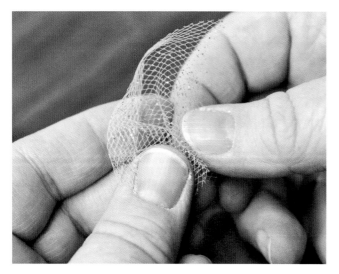

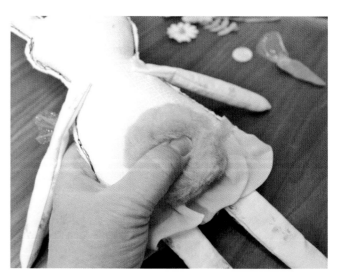

5. Gather a small scrap of green tulle with your fingers and hot glue it to the top of the carrots. Trim off the excess tulle if needed. One carrot goes in Daisy's pocket, and the other carrot can be safety pinned onto her hand.

6. Hot glue a big pink pom-pom onto her backside for a tail.

7. Cut a piece of lace and glue it around her neck. Glue a big pink button over the lace collar.

8. Arrange flowers and leaves on the bunny doll's head in a pleasing manner and hot glue in place.

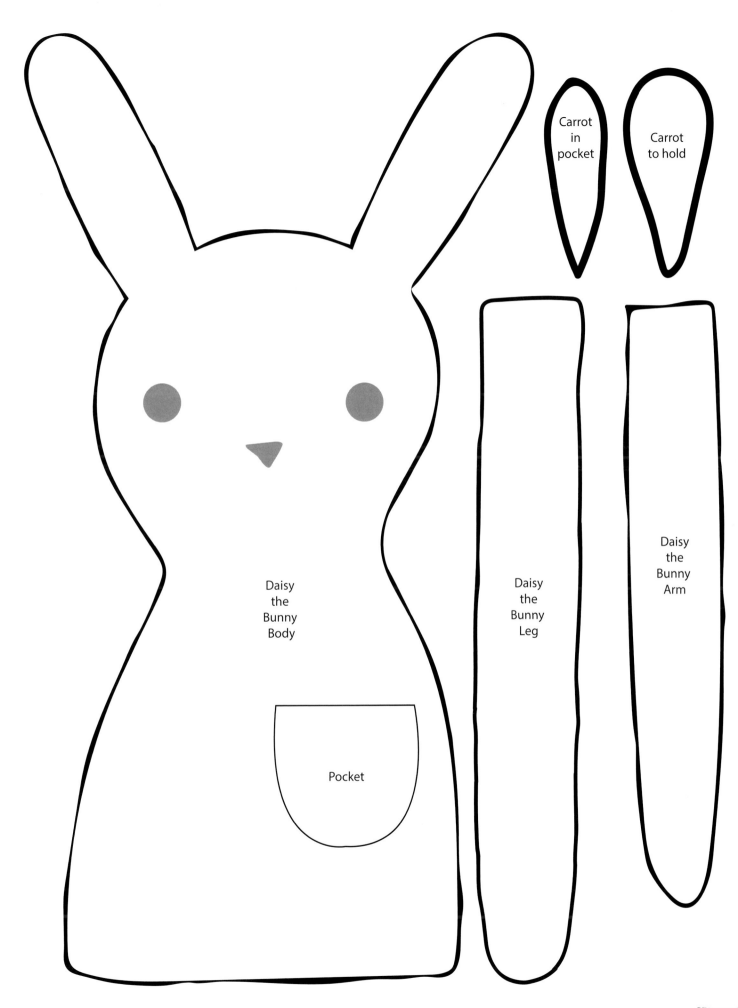

Carrot
in
pocket

Carrot
to hold

Daisy
the
Bunny
Body

Daisy
the
Bunny
Leg

Daisy
the
Bunny
Arm

Pocket

DErRICK THE HALLOWEEN VAMPIRE

On a dark and spooky night, Derrick Dracula meets up with his ghoulish friends. He is dressed in his party cape, is wearing his count medal, and holds a not-so-scary pumpkin sign. This sweet guy is very blue, but his face is friendly. Let the fun begin!

Materials

Muslin: 8″ × 12″

Coordinating fabric scraps for arms and legs: 8″ × 10″ for each set

Fabric scrap for back of doll: 8″ × 12″

Black silk or satin for cape: 22″ × 10″

Fabric scrap for pocket

Ribbon, yarn, and trim scraps

Pencil

Black thread

Stuffing for dolls and stuff-it tool

Acrylic paint: Light blue, hot pink, black, medium blue, white, yellow, and purple

Paintbrushes: Large and small

Colored pencils: Black, dark blue, red, pink, blue, light green, and yellow

Pastels: White, blue, and purple

Hot glue gun and glue sticks

Buttons: 1 large black and 1 large silver

Orange glitter

Clear-drying glue

Black perle cotton or heavy thread

Halloween ephemera (paper pumpkin, felt bat, party streamer scrap, and "Be Afraid" saying) **and straw for sign**

Fixative spray

Drawing the Doll

Refer to Draw the Doll on Muslin (page 8).

1. Make a paper pattern using the Derrick the Halloween Vampire body pattern (page 47). Place it on the muslin and trace with a pencil all the way around.

2. Place the traced muslin doll onto the backing fabric, wrong sides together, and pin.

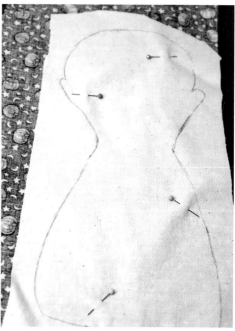

Finished doll:
7″ × 16½″

Photo by Shirley Hudson

Sewing the Doll

Refer to Primitive Sewing: Head and Body (page 9).

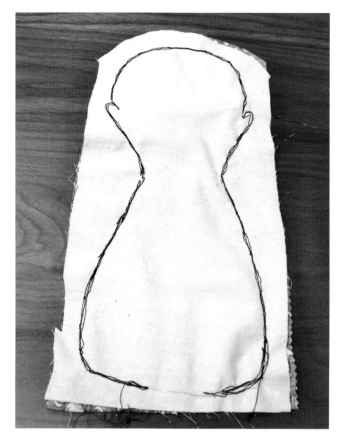

1. Primitively sew the head and body on the traced line around the vampire shape, leaving a 3″ opening at the bottom of the doll. Sew around the ear shape.

2. Trim around the vampire doll ⅛″ away from the sewing line. Stuff the vampire doll firmly, especially in the neck area. Sew the opening on the vampire doll closed.

3. Lightly mark the facial features (eyes, nose, mouth, and hair) with a pencil.

The Base of the Head and Body

Refer to Base of the Head, Hair, and Body (page 10).

1. Paint the vampire's face and ears using a lightly watered-down light blue. While the face is still wet, add hot pink to the cheeks. Add a small amount of hot pink to the nose area and mouth. The pink color will blend into the blue, creating a soft look. Let dry.

2. Paint the vampire's hair black. Paint small sideburns near the ears.

3. Paint the vampire's torso black. Let dry.

The Face

Refer to Eyes, Nose, Mouth, and Hair (page 11).

1. Paint the eyes following the eye painting guide below.

• Paint a black circle. Let dry.

• Paint a smaller medium-blue circle to create an iris. Let dry.

• Paint a small black circle for a pupil. Let dry.

• Add white highlights to the eye. Let dry.

• Add flecks of color in the iris with a darker blue colored pencil.

2. Paint the nose following the nose painting guide at right.

• Paint the nose pink.

• Paint the top of the nose yellow.

3. Paint the mouth following the mouth painting guide at right.

• Paint the mouth pink.

Eye painting guide

Nose painting guide

Mouth painting guide

4. Apply pink and yellow colored pencils to the nose for more intense color.

Tip: Layering

Layering paint, colored pencils, and pastels on your dolls make the features seem less flat. It adds dimension, texture, and shadows to the features of your doll's face. Adding blue or green around areas like the nose, mouth, and face makes the curvatures pop, producing a face that looks more realistic.

5. Outline the eyes and color around the outer areas of the nose with a blue colored pencil.

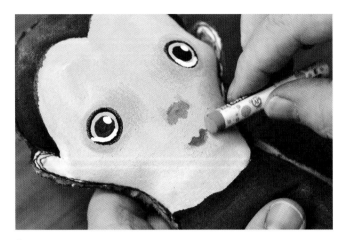

6. Apply blue pastel to the inner areas of the eyes to create shadow and depth. Also use blue pastel on the sides of the nose to create shadows.

7. Use blue pastel on the sides of the mouth and under the sides of the lips.

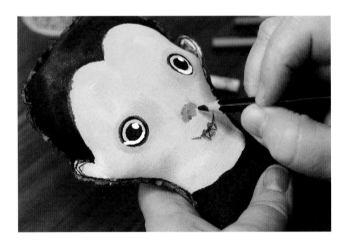

8. Using a black colored pencil, draw the mouth into a smile over the lips. Add teeth by the lower lip with a black colored pencil.

9. Add nostrils and shadows under the nose with black colored pencil.

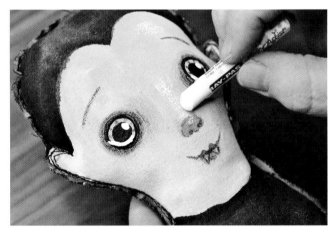

10. Using a black colored pencil, add eyebrows to the face and spooky dark circles around his eyes. Add longer sideburns if needed.

11. Apply white pastel to the bridge of the nose and the tip of the nose to create a highlight. Apply dark blue colored pencil to the inner eyes.

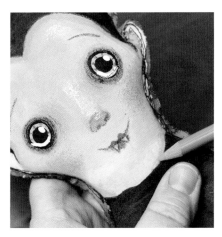

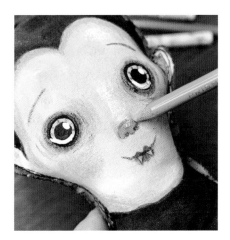

12. Add red to the lips using a colored pencil. Lightly apply pink colored pencil to the cheeks.

13. Use a blue colored pencil to shade around the face, hairline, and neck.

14. Shade around the upper hairline using a dark blue colored pencil. Blending shades of colors really makes the doll come to life. Apply black colored pencil under the eyes to make him look old.

15. Apply light green colored pencil to the face around the outer cheeks, hairline, and nose.

16. Using white pastel, draw on the middle part of his hair and streaks to represent combed hair.

17. Add some lines over the eyes area, around the outer eyes, along the side of the nose, and under the mouth using a yellow colored pencil.

Tip: Correcting Mistakes
To correct a painting mistake, simply paint over the error or use a pastel to cover it up. Don't worry about imperfections; sometimes it becomes what the doll needs most!

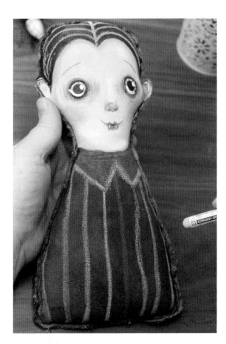

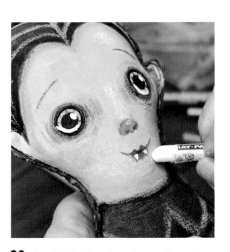

18. Draw a collar on the black torso using a purple pastel, and fill in the whole collar area. Add a long line of purple from the collar to the bottom of the torso.

19. Add stripes to his outfit using a light blue pastel. Add blue pastel under his collar.

20. Apply black colored pencil to the vampire doll's neck by the collar, and add a light line for a chin. Paint the teeth white with white paint and a small brush. Let dry. Add a few lines of white pastel around the chin. Spray with fixative to set the paint, pencil, and pastel.

Sewing the Arms and Legs

Refer to Arms and Legs (page 14).

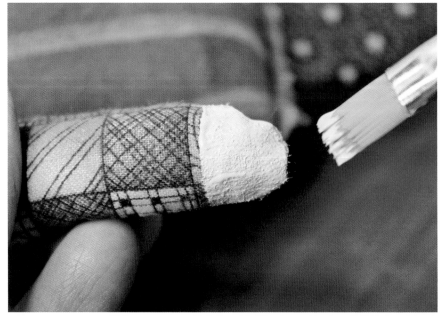

1. Make the arms and legs for the vampire doll.

2. Hot glue the arms and legs to the vampire doll.

3. Paint Derrick's hands blue and the feet purple. Let dry.

Finishing Derrick the Halloween Vampire

Refer to Embellishing (page 15).

1. To make a count medal, choose a large button, a clear glue, and glitter. Add glitter to the button and let dry.

2. Cut 1 pocket from Halloween fabric and hot glue it onto the vampire doll, leaving the top open. Add glitter trim to the top of the pocket using hot glue.

3. Take a length of scrunched seam binding or ribbon, and tie a bow around his neck. Glue on a silver button just underneath the bow.

NOTE ■ Scrunched seam binding is seam binding that has been dunked in hot water, scrunched into a ball, and left to dry in a ball. It will have a really nice crinkled look.

4. Cut 2 pieces of purple ribbon 2½″ long. Hot glue the 2 ribbons to the back of the count medal so the ribbons dangle below the button. Hot glue the count medal onto the vampire doll's chest.

5. Cut a piece of black satin 22″ × 10″. Using a 20″ piece of black perle cotton thread and a needle, sew a gathering stitch 1½″ from the edge of the 22″ length. Gather the cape at the center of the thread.

6. Gather fun Halloween ephemera to make a sign for Derrick to hold or put in his pocket. Use a 5″ long straw or stick. Hot glue a pumpkin, bat, scrunched party streamer, and saying to the top of the straw.

7. Hot glue ribbon to the bottom of the vampire doll's torso, above the legs.

8. Hot glue yarn trim around the arms by the hands and around the legs by the feet. Place the cape around the vampire doll's neck and tie the perle cotton into a bow.

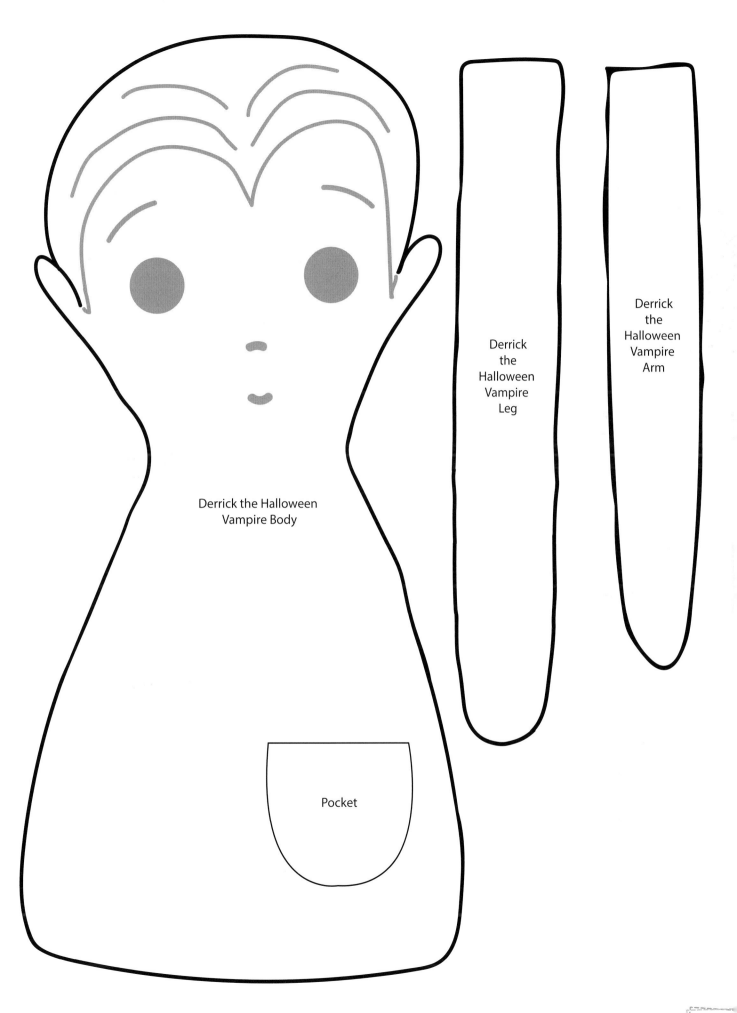

Derrick the Halloween Vampire Body

Derrick the Halloween Vampire Leg

Derrick the Halloween Vampire Arm

Pocket

SPARKLES THE SNOWMAN

Wintertime can be cold and harsh, but not for Sparkles. She loves the icicles, frosty temps, and snowball fights. Her love for playing never stops her from being outside. Sparkles has a carrot nose and big blue eyes, plus a wool hat and scarf to keep her cozy. Make a snowman to represent each member of your family!

Materials

Muslin: 8″ × 12″

Fabric scrap for back of doll: 8″ × 12″

Plaid wool/felt scraps for scarf and hat

Twigs for arms: 2 about 6″ long (Twigs that have 2 or 3 offshoots are best because the ends look like hands or fingers.)

Pencil

Black thread

Stuffing for dolls and stuff-it tool

Acrylic paint: White, pink, gray, black, blue, orange, and caramel

Paintbrushes: Large and small

Colored pencils: Blue, gray, black, red, and green

Pastels: Gray, orange, and red

Hot glue gun and glue sticks

Red fringy-yarn trim for hat

Glittery pom-poms: 1 red and 1 white, ¾″ or 1″ diameter

Buttons: 3 small to medium red

Iridescent glitter

Clear-drying glue

Fixative spray

Drawing the Doll

Refer to Draw the Doll on Muslin (page 8).

1. Make a paper pattern using the Sparkles the Snowman body pattern (page 55). Place it on the muslin and trace with a pencil all the way around.

2. Place the traced muslin doll onto the backing fabric, wrong sides together, and pin.

3. The snowman has a carrot nose. Place the snowman nose pattern on muslin and trace around the shape. Place another fabric under the traced nose. Pin together.

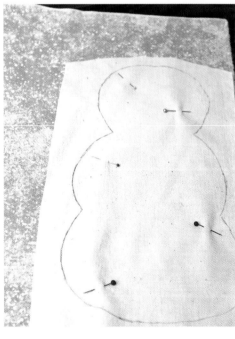

Finished doll:
14½″ × 11″
including twig arms

Photo by Shirley Hudson

Sewing the Doll

Refer to Primitive Sewing: Head and Body (page 9).

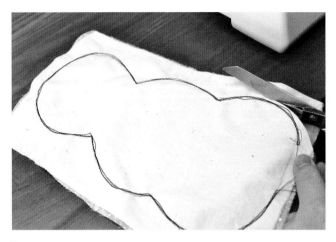

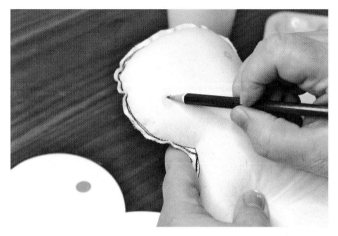

1. Primitively sew the head and body on the traced line around the snowman shape, leaving a 3˝ opening at the bottom of the doll. Also sew around the snowman nose.

2. Trim around the snowman and nose ⅛˝ away from the sewing line.

3. Stuff the snowman doll firmly, especially in the neck area. Leave the nose flat and unstuffed. Sew the opening on the snowman doll closed.

4. Lightly mark the eyes on the face with a pencil.

The Base of the Head and Body

Refer to Base of the Head, Hair, and Body (page 10).

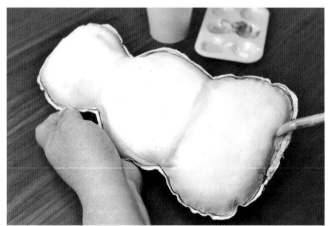

1. Paint the snowman's face and torso using a lightly watered-down white. While the face is still wet, add pink to the cheeks. The pink color will blend into the white, creating a soft look. Let dry.

2. Apply watered-down gray paint to the outer edges of the snowman, near the stitched lines. This creates depth. Also add gray under the face, by the neckline, and under the belly.

The Face

Refer to Eyes, Nose, Mouth, and Hair (page 11).

1. Paint the eyes following the eye painting guide below.

• Paint a black circle. Let dry.

• Paint a smaller blue circle to create an iris. Let dry.

• Paint a small black circle for a pupil. Let dry.

• Add white highlights to the eye. Let dry.

• Add flecks of color in the iris with a darker blue colored pencil.

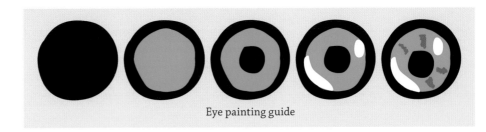

Eye painting guide

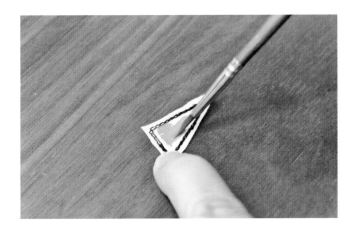

2. Paint the nose with lightly watered-down orange. Let dry.

3. Paint the lips/mouth on the snowman doll, directing the ends of the smile upward. Give a boy snowman a less pink option, like caramel paint.

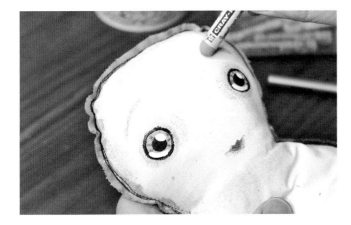

4. Apply gray colored pencil around the eyes and nose. Use gray pastel on the inner areas of the eyes, towards the center of the face. Apply gray pastel under the mouth and draw on the eyebrows.

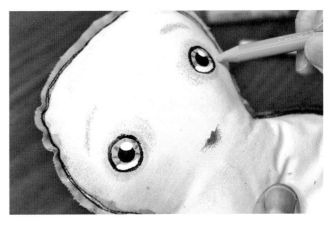

5. Add blue to the inner areas of the eyes using a colored pencil. Apply blue colored pencil to the side edges, to the neckline, to the belly line, and under the mouth of Sparkles.

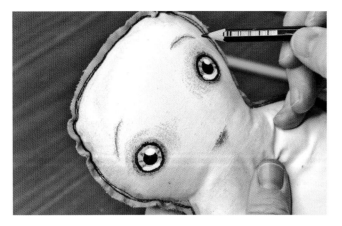 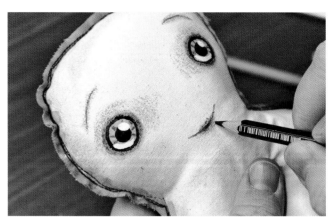

6. Use black colored pencil around the eyes. Draw over the eyebrows using black pencil to help define them.

7. Using a black colored pencil, add a smile and a small smudge between the lips so they look like they are opening just a bit. Define under the lips with a black pencil. Apply a red colored pencil to the lips, if needed.

 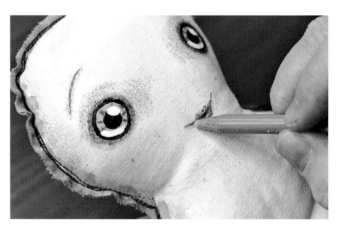

8. Add color to the carrot nose using orange pastels. Add lines on the carrot using black colored pencil.

9. Add light green colored pencil to the outer and inner areas of the eyes and around the mouth. Add green to the curves on snowman. Blue and green make the doll feel more rounded.

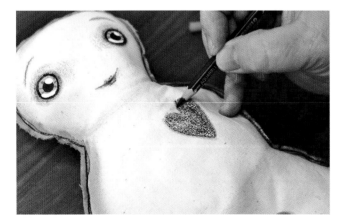

10. Draw a heart on the chest using red pastel. Outline the heart using a black colored pencil.

11. Spray with fixative to set the paint, pencil, and pastel.

The Arms and Nose

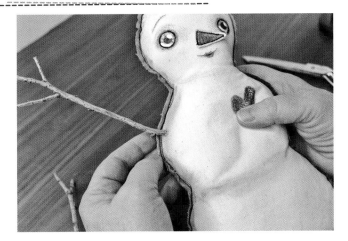

1. Hot glue the nose onto the face.

2. Hold the twig arms up to the snowman doll. Decide where they should go and how long you want them to be.

3. Cut a small slit in the snowman for each twig arm.

4. Trim the twigs to size. *Note:* There should be at least 1˝ of the branch inside the snowman doll. Hot glue the arms in place. Make sure to put plenty of glue in the hole of the slit and to hold the arm in place until it sets.

Finishing Sparkles the Snowman

Refer to Embellishing (page 15).

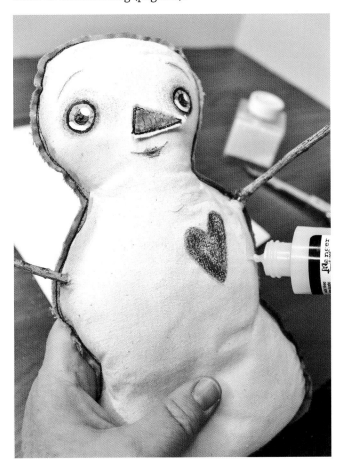

1. For a frosty look, spread lines of clear tacky glue over the head, nose, chest, sides, and anywhere you want her to glisten. Sprinkle glitter over the glue and shake the excess off. Let dry.

2. Cut a scarf ¾˝ × 17˝ from wool or felt. Trim the ends of the scarf to make a fringe. Wrap the scarf around the neck and tie.

3. Using the snowman hat pattern, cut out a hat from wool/felt. Hot glue a red pom-pom on the top of the hat.

4. Hot glue the hat to the top of the snowman doll's head.

5. Glue the fringy-yarn trim to the hat in many layers.

6. Hot glue a white pom-pom to the snowman doll's hand.

7. Hot glue 3 red buttons to the torso, from smallest to largest.

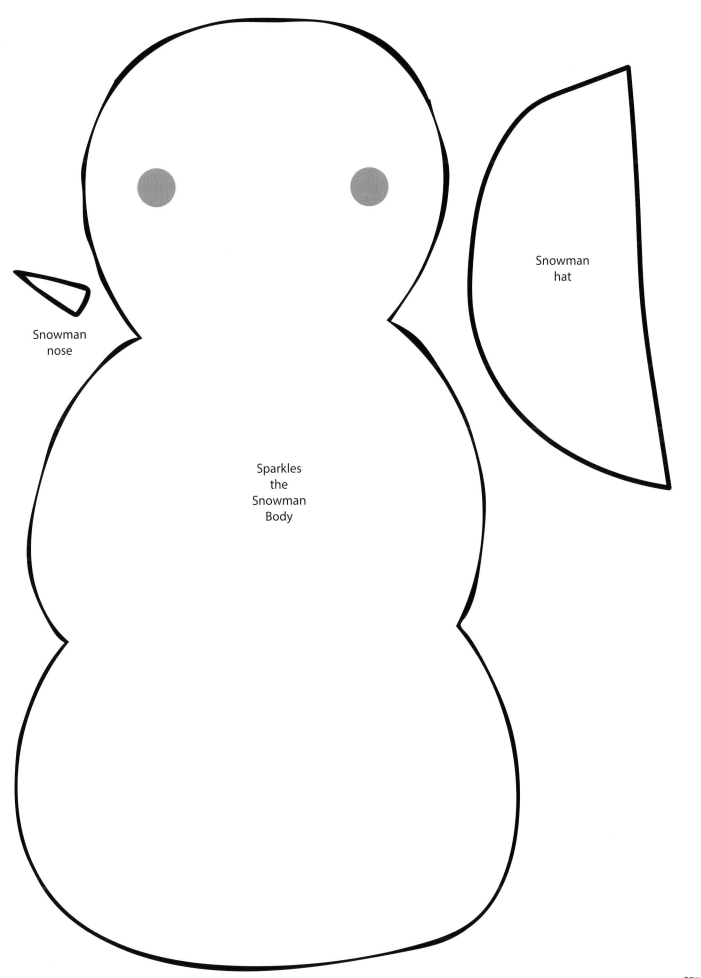

Snowman hat

Snowman nose

Sparkles
the
Snowman
Body

Gallery of Dolls
Pictures to Inspire

By Shirley Hudson

A good friend asked for a Frida doll, so I researched her. Frida Kahlo, the artist, has black hair piled up on her head. She wears flowers, scarves, and jewelry. I really looked in my stash of supplies and found a lot I could use. Her skirt is bright and something she would love. She is holding a paintbrush. My daughter Selina made me a tiny palette from wood.

Frida has some three-dimensional flowers on her head, and she also has a hint of a unibrow. Her earrings are jewelry-supply jump rings.

Photo by Shirley Hudson

By Shirley Hudson

Lady Liberty represents a very patriotic Statue of Liberty. She has a crown, torch, and flag. Her dress was made from scraps of 6″-wide red, white, and blue tulle. Each piece of tulle was tied in a knot and hot glued in place in alternating colors. After all the tulle got around, it ended up looking like a tutu! The torch is hand drawn on muslin, primitively stitched, and then painted.

The crown was drawn on muslin at the same time as the doll shape. They are connected. Adding glitter to the crown adds a touch of sparkle.

Photo by Shirley Hudson

By Shirley Hudson

Uncle Sam has a fun hat, bow tie, lots of silver embellishments, a flag, and a patriotic pocket with a stamp inside.

This patriotic gentleman also has a triangle beard and a crocheted bow tie.

Photo by Shirley Hudson

By Shirley Hudson

This lucky leprechaun has many embellishments: a shamrock on his hat, a crochet clover in one hand (which I learned how to make on a YouTube video), and a felt rainbow in the other hand (made using a few scraps of U-shaped felt that were glued on top of a purple background).

His mustache and beard is a bit of chunky wool yarn. The bow tie is green tulle tied in a knot. In his pocket are some gold coins from old jewelry scraps.

Photo by Shirley Hudson

By Shirley Hudson

The pilgrim is less embellished because pilgrims wore plain outfits. She does have a satin dress, which is really a long scrap of satin gathered on one side with a running stitch. The dress was hot glued on the doll. She is holding the turkey (page 27).

Her hat was drawn on muslin when I drew her face and torso. I used white pastel to create a faux pocket.

Give Thanks

Photo by Shirley Hudson

By Shirley Hudson

This cat has striped legs, fringy yarn around her neck to look like a mane, and a fun felt pumpkin.

I made lines and marks on the doll with colored pencils to mimic fur. Her sign says, "Meow is the time for pumpkin spice."

Meow is the time for pumpkin Spice!

Photo by Shirley Hudson

By Selina Hudson

Anime and manga are very popular—try making one of these characters! Paint fun products on your doll's torso. This doll was hand drawn on muslin and is more slender than the other dolls.

Try different eye shapes and more white highlights in the eyes. Her hair has a lot of stitching, making it fun and unique.

Photo by Shirley Hudson

By Selina Hudson

This pirate is ready to reach Davy Jones's locker. He has a pirate hat, big brown eyes, and felt boots.

His underneath hair was painted, but there is a top layer of brown yarn to give him the dreadlock look. Selina attached beads in the hair and beard for a very modern pirate.

Photo by Shirley Hudson

By Selina Hudson

The Mad Hatter is a very fun doll. He has lace at his throat with a big brooch (formerly an earring), more lace for cuffs, and the sweetest teacup.

His wild hair is the best. It was heavily stitched and painted orange. The lips are big and thick. The eyes are green, and I love the highlights of white. His nose is mainly some gray paint, and I love the red/pink around the eyes.

Photo by Shirley Hudson

By Selina Hudson

A flat doll, this forest deer has the kawaii-eyed look. It was drawn on muslin, stitched, lightly stuffed, and painted. The paint makes the doll stiff. It can have a hanger on the back to display it on the wall.

Kawaii eyes are so dreamy and can be very simple like these. Lines of colored pencil give a furry look on the face.

Photo by Shirley Hudson

By Shirley Hudson

The Bride of Frankenstein, alive!
She has a very simple dress: It's just a
white gauze fabric, running stitched
along one side, gathered at the neck, and
glued to secure. Her arms have creepy
fingers and she needs a diamond ring
(she is engaged to Frankie).

I stitched her hair when I was making her
head; it is lightly stuffed. Her pin is a bolt
of lightning—really a piece of cardboard
with glitter. The bride has a few scars,
drawn on using a red permanent pen.

She's Alive!

Photo by Shirley Hudson

By Shirley Hudson

Frankenstein's monster is so innocent and not scary at all. He was painted a nice shade of green. His pants are formal stripes, and he has spider-fabric arms and a fun pocket of eyeballs.

His hair, nose, and lips have a nice shine, courtesy of a bit of white pastel. I learned how to crochet a few things recently—one being the bow tie, to the back of which I added a pin back. He holds a sign of assorted ephemera. Sometimes the more you add, the better the doll looks.

Photo by Shirley Hudson

october

By Shirley Hudson

The Creature from the Black Lagoon is made of cool green batik fabric and creepy stitched hands and feet. Fringy yarn and green-dyed cheesecloth strips were hung on his neck and hands. He became very swampy! His gills and fins on the shoulder were drawn on muslin, stitched, and painted green.

His nose and scales were drawn using black colored pencil. I added a crocheted heart on him because he loved the girl!

Photo by Shirley Hudson

DEEP FROM THE SWAMP, HE WAITS FOR A BEAUTY

By Shirley Hudson

I've made at least ten werewolves; each one ends up looking a little different from the other. They all are fun and imaginative. I like to make the pants in a Swinging Sixties look by choosing just the right kind of fabric for the legs. Wolfy's shirt has a denim look and fringy yarn is perfect for his hairy chest, plus the arms and legs.

Wolfy's hair is stitched on the outer areas and painted on the inner head areas, too. Try looking at photos of creatures you want to make and notice their features. Wolfy has a doglike snout and teeth.

BEWARE OF THE FULL MOON!

Photo by Shirley Hudson

By Shirley Hudson

For Skelly, I painted the face like a skull with cracks and teeth. His big blue eyes make him not so scary. He has a silvery tulle bow tie.

Use rickrack down the arms and legs to create the look of bones. Add black fringy yarn to his hands and white pom-poms for trim by his legs, and make a fun sign out of papers for him to hold.

Photo by Shirley Hudson

By Shirley Hudson

Pumpkins can have happy, spooky, cute, goofy, or scary faces. Pumpkin Man is my country bumpkin. White freckles give him an innocent look. He has green tulle at his neck, green fringy yarn down his body, a fun sign, and pom-pom trim!

This pumpkin is scary just by adding a red mouth and teeth! White pastels give him a shine. He has a small vine by his neck that was stitched on muslin when making the doll.

Photo by Shirley Hudson

Gallery of Dolls—Pictures to Inspire

By Shirley Hudson

The mummy is unique! The idea is to make it look like it is wrapped. I used strips of coffee-stained cheesecloth to wrap the doll; then I hot glued the strips in place. A big wool heart is safety pinned in place.

The piercing blue eyes really show up through the bandages. Shading with beige, yellow, white, and grays really adds to the ancient feel. Again, this monster isn't scary. A smile usually softens any doll. Frowns and furrowed eyebrows create anger or meanness.

Photo by Shirley Hudson

DON'T
MAKE ME
DROP A
HOUSE
ON YOU

By Shirley Hudson

Witches are so much fun! You can paint their skin green, give them a broom and fancy ballerina shoes, and use black tulle on the hat. You can make them frightening or friendly.

This witch has a cool cape, a bow on her hat, orange hair, and a fun sign to hold. Each witch can look completely different.

Photo by
Shirley Hudson

By Shirley Hudson

Zombie girl has very deep black eyes with lots of black colored-pencil shading around them. (It gives the dead look.) I made some brains (zombies *love* brains) using pink fabric placed on cotton batting with lots of free-motion stitching. I squiggled back and forth with the stitching until it looked like a brain.

Splattering watered-down paint on the dolls is a fun way to make them look old or vintage. She really is rough and primitive, but I think she needs to be rough to be a zombie. Her pin was made from cut-up party streamers and Halloween papers, with some ribbons dangling down.

Photo by Shirley Hudson

By Shirley Hudson

This black widow has her eggs (pom-poms), lots of legs, and a red hourglass on her torso.

I added fringy yarn for a hairy look and a pearl necklace. (She's fancy!) I made her eyes a little goofy for fun.

POISON

POISON

Photo by Shirley Hudson

Photo by Shirley Hudson

GOING
BATTY,
FOR
YOUR
BLOOD!

By Shirley Hudson

This bat is especially goofy (but cute!) with his big head and little wings. A complementary color to black is blue, so I added quite a bit.

I also added black fringy yarn for a hairy look, black glitter on the wings, blue yarn around the neck, and sweet little fangs.

By Selina Hudson

This fun character has a striped painted outfit, wildly green hair, green-dyed cheesecloth bits glued to his face and neck, and fun blue eyes.

He has many layers of shading on his face, and his hair is crazy stiff from the stitching and paint.

Photo by Shirley Hudson

HANDBOOK FOR THE
Recently
Deceased

By Selina Hudson

This classic vampire has a striped suit, small cape, upper-crust metal, and intense brown eyes.

I love his hair; the bangs are wispy yet styled. He has a cravat around his throat. The layers of shading are fun and really make him stand out.

Photo by Shirley Hudson